First edition

Jack and Jill

and other nursery rhymes

Illustrated by KEN McKIE

Ladybird Books Loughborough

*J*ack and Jill went up the hill
To fetch a pail of water;
Jack fell down and broke his crown,
And Jill came tumbling after.

Up Jack got, and home did trot,
As fast as he could caper,
He went to bed to mend his head,
With vinegar and brown paper.

Wee Willie Winkie
 runs through the town,

Upstairs and downstairs
 in his nightgown,

Knocking on the window,
 crying through the lock,

Are the children all in bed,
 it's past eight-o'clock?

This little pig went to market,
This little pig stayed at home,
This little pig had roast beef,
This little pig had none,
And this little pig
cried "Wee-wee-wee,"
all the way home.

There was an old woman
              tossed up in a basket,

Seventeen times as high as the moon;

Where she was going
              I couldn't but ask her,

For in her hand she carried a broom.

Old woman, old woman, old woman,
                          quoth I,

Where are you going to up so high?

To brush the cobwebs off the sky!

May I go with you?

Yes, by-and-by.

Cock a doodle doo!
My dame has lost her shoe,
My master's lost his fiddling stick,
And doesn't know what to do.

Pussy cat, pussy cat,
where have you been?

I've been to London
to look at the queen.

Pussy cat, pussy cat,
what did you there?

I frightened a little mouse
under a chair.

Polly put the kettle on,
Polly put the kettle on,
Polly put the kettle on,
  We'll all have some tea.

Sukey take it off again,
Sukey take it off again,
Sukey take it off again,
  They've all gone away.

Hey diddle diddle,
The cat and the fiddle,
The cow jumped over the moon;
The little dog laughed
To see such fun,
And the dish ran away
      with the spoon.

Little Tommy Tittlemouse
Lived in a little house;
He caught fishes
In other men's ditches.

I love little pussy,
Her coat is so warm,

And if I don't hurt her
She'll do me no harm.

So I'll not pull her tail,
Nor drive her away,

But pussy and I
Very gently will play.

I had a little nut tree,
Nothing would it bear
But a silver nutmeg
And a golden pear.

The King of Spain's daughter
Came to visit me,
And all for the sake
Of my little nut tree.

*Little Bo-Peep
has lost her sheep,*

*And doesn't know
where to find them;*

*Leave them alone
and they'll come home,*

Wagging their tails behind them.

Peter, Peter, pumpkin eater,
Had a wife and couldn't keep her;
He put her in a pumpkin shell
And there he kept her very well.

One, two, three, four, five,
Once I caught a fish alive.
Six, seven, eight, nine, ten,
Then I let it go again.

Why did you let it go?
Because it bit my finger so.
Which finger did it bite?
This little finger on the right.

Little Polly Flinders
Sat among the cinders,
Warming her pretty little toes;
Her mother came and caught her,
And whipped her little daughter
For spoiling her nice new clothes.

*L*ittle Boy Blue,

Come blow your horn,

The sheep's in the meadow,

The cow's in the corn.

But where is the boy

Who looks after the sheep?

He's under a haycock,

Fast asleep.

Will you wake him?

No, not I,

For if I do,

He's sure to cry.

Oh! The grand old Duke of York,

He had ten thousand men;

He marched them up
to the top of the hill,

And he marched them down again.

And when they were up they were up,

And when they were down
they were down,

And when they were only half-way up,

They were neither up nor down.

Ding, dong, bell,
Pussy's in the well.
Who put her in?
Little Johnny Green.
Who pulled her out?
Little Tommy Stout.

What a naughty boy was that,
To try to drown poor pussy cat,
Who never did him any harm,
And killed the mice in his
            father's barn.

Sing a song of sixpence,
A pocket full of rye;
Four and twenty blackbirds,
Baked in a pie.

When the pie was opened,
The birds began to sing;
Now wasn't that a dainty dish,
To set before the king?

The king was in his counting-house,
Counting out his money;
The queen was in the parlour,
Eating bread and honey.

The maid was in the garden,
Hanging out the clothes,
When down came a blackbird,
And pecked off her nose.

Bobby Shaftoe's gone to sea,
Silver buckles on his knee;
He'll come back and marry me,
Bonny Bobby Shaftoe!

Bobby Shaftoe's fat and fair,
Combing down his yellow hair.
He's my love for ever more
Bonny Bobby Shaftoe!